Positive

AFFIRMATIONS

for Women

M. M Adina

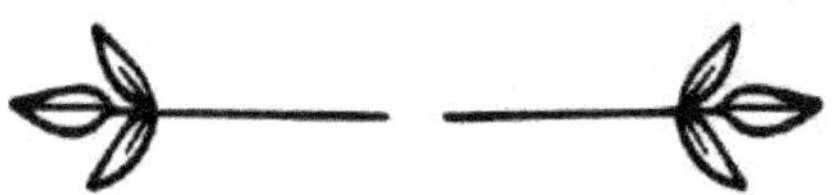

"Positive Affirmations for Women" is a self-help book that
aims to empower women by providing them with a collectic
of positive affirmations that they can use to boost their
confidence, motivation, and self-esteem. The book is writte
by various authors and contains a wide range of affirmatio
that cover different areas of life, such as relationships,
career, health, and spirituality.

The book begins by explaining what affirmations are and h
they can be used to change negative thought patterns and
beliefs. It then goes on to provide a large number of
affirmations that readers can use to help them overcome se
doubt, fear, and anxiety, and to cultivate a positive and
confident mindset.

The affirmations in the book are designed to be simple, cle
and easy to remember, and they are organized into differe
categories based on the areas of life they address. Each
affirmation is accompanied by a brief explanation of why
is effective and how it can be used in daily life.

Overall, "Positive Affirmations for Women" is a practical an
uplifting book that can help women develop a positive
mindset and overcome self-limiting beliefs. It is an exceller
resource for women who want to improve their self-esteem
achieve their goals, and live a happier and more fulfilling
life.

POSITIVE AFFIRMATIONS IN THE FOLLOWING CATEGORIES:

- Positive Mindset
- Abundance
- Self-love/self-worth
- -ConfidenceGratitude
- Motivation
- Healing
- Positive Mindset
- Success & Money
- Relationship

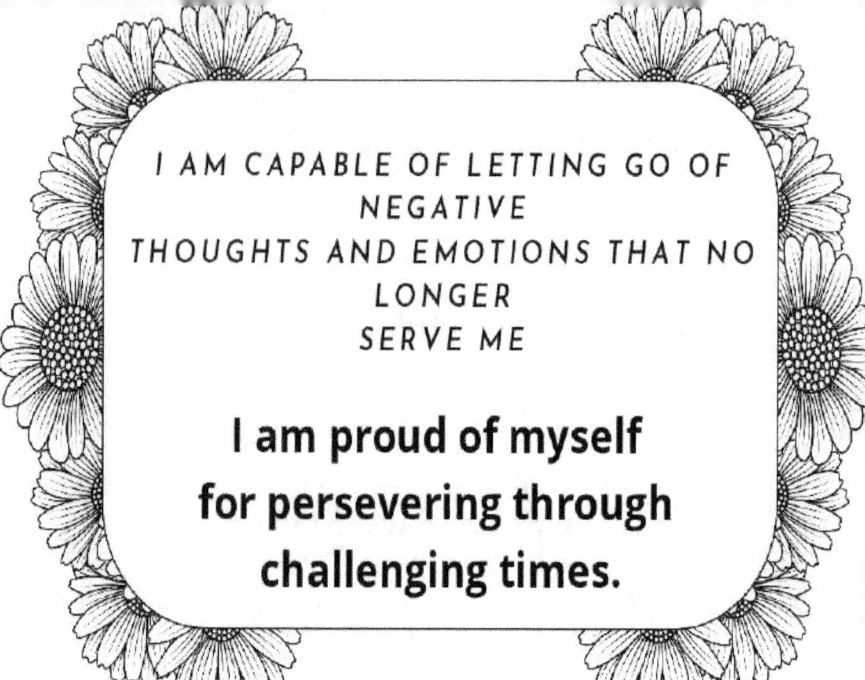

I AM DESERVING OF SELF-LOVE AND
SELF ACCEPTANCE, JUST AS I AM.

I AM CONFIDENT IN MY ABILITY TO
HANDLE
WHATEVER OBSTACLES COME MY WAY

I TRUST IN MY ABILITY TO MAKE THE
RIGHT DECISIONS FOR MYSELF.

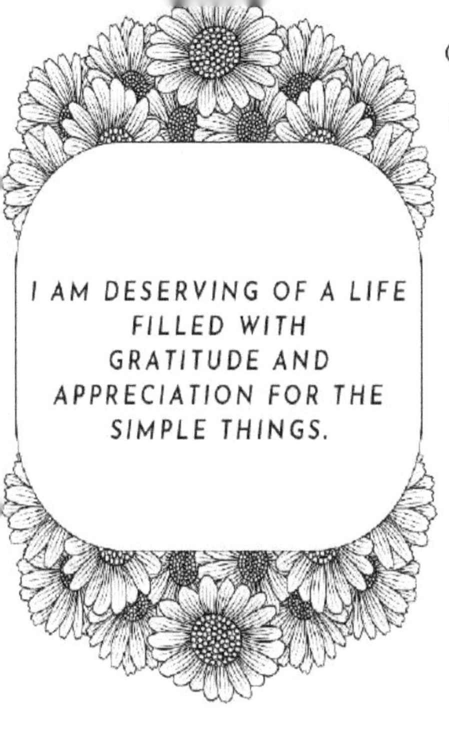

I am confident in my ability to pursue my passions and live a fulfilling life.

I AM DESERVING OF A LIFE FILLED WITH GRATITUDE AND APPRECIATION FOR THE SIMPLE THINGS.

I am deserving of a life filled with love, joy, and abundance.

I am grateful for my physical and emotional health and wellbeing.

I AM WORTHY AND DESERVING OF LOVE AND RESPECT.

I am proud of myself for taking steps towards achieving my goals and dreams.

I am capable of building a supportive community of people who uplift and inspire me.

I AM CAPABLE OF CREATING
A POSITIVE
IMPACT IN THE WORLD
AND LEAVING A
LEGACY THAT INSPIRES OTHER

I AM GRATEFUL FOR THE OPPORTUNITIES TO LEARN AND GROW FROM MY EXPERIENCES.

I AM CONFIDENT IN MY ABILITY TO FIND SOLUTIONS TO ANY CHALLENGE THAT ARISES.

I AM DESERVING OF A LIFE FILLED WITH ADVENTURE AND NEW EXPERIENCES.

I AM CAPABLE OF CREATING A LIFE THAT ALIGNS WITH MY VALUES AND BELIEFS.

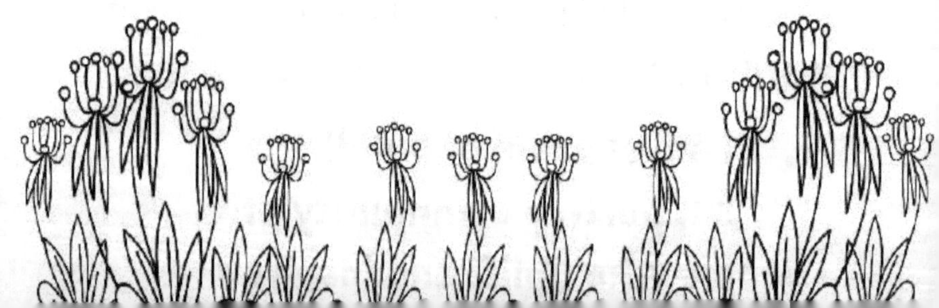

I AM PROUD OF MY
UNIQUE TALENTS AND
GIFTS THAT
MAKE ME WHO I AM

I AM GRATEFUL FOR MY JOURNEY
AND ITS LESSONS.

I AM IN FULL CONTROL OF MY LIFE.

I AM CONFIDENT IN MY ABILITY TO SPEAK
Y TRUTH WITH AUTHENTICITY AND CLARITY.

I am capable of practicing self compassion and treating myself with kindness and understanding.

I am deserving of healthy and supportive
relationships that uplift and inspire me

I AM GRATEFUL FOR THE BEAUTY AND
WONDER OF THE NATURAL WORLD AROUND
ME

I AM CONFIDENT IN MY ABILITY TO MAKE A POSITIVE IMPACT ON THE WORLD.

I AM DESERVING OF RESPECT AND ADMIRATION FOR MY ACHIEVEMENTS AND CONTRIBUTIONS.

I AM PROUD OF MYSELF FOR STANDING UP FOR WHAT I BELIEVE IN AND FIGHTING FOR JUSTICE AND EQUALITY.

I AM CAPABLE OF EMBRACING CHANGE AND ADAPTING TO NEW SITUATIONS WITH EASE.

I AM CONFIDENT IN MY ABILITY TO LEARN NEW SKILLS AND EXPAND MY KNOWLEDGE.

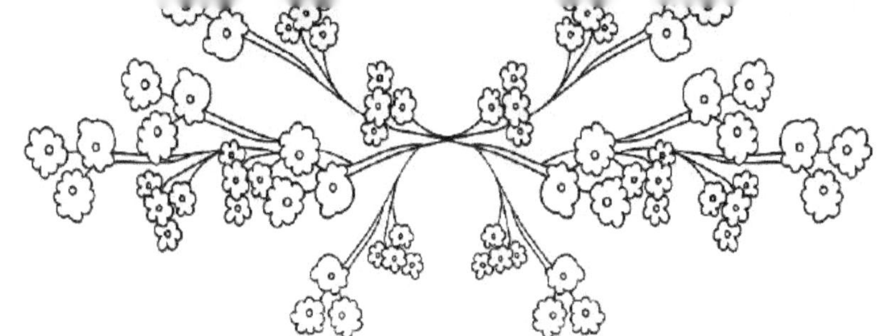

I AM CONFIDENT IN MY ABILITY TO MAKE DECISIONS THAT ALIGN WITH MY VALUES AND BRING ME CLOSER TO MY GOALS.

I AM CONFIDENT IN MY ABILITY TO HANDLE ANY SITUATION WITH GRACE AND RESILIENCE.

I AM DESERVING OF A LIFE FILLED WITH ABUNDANCE, PROSPERITY, AND FULFILLMENT.

I AM CAPABLE OF ACHIEVING MY GOALS AND DREAMS THROUGH HARD WORK AND DETERMINATION.

I AM GRATEFUL FOR THE SUPPORTIVE AND UPLIFTING COMMUNITY OF WOMEN AROUND ME

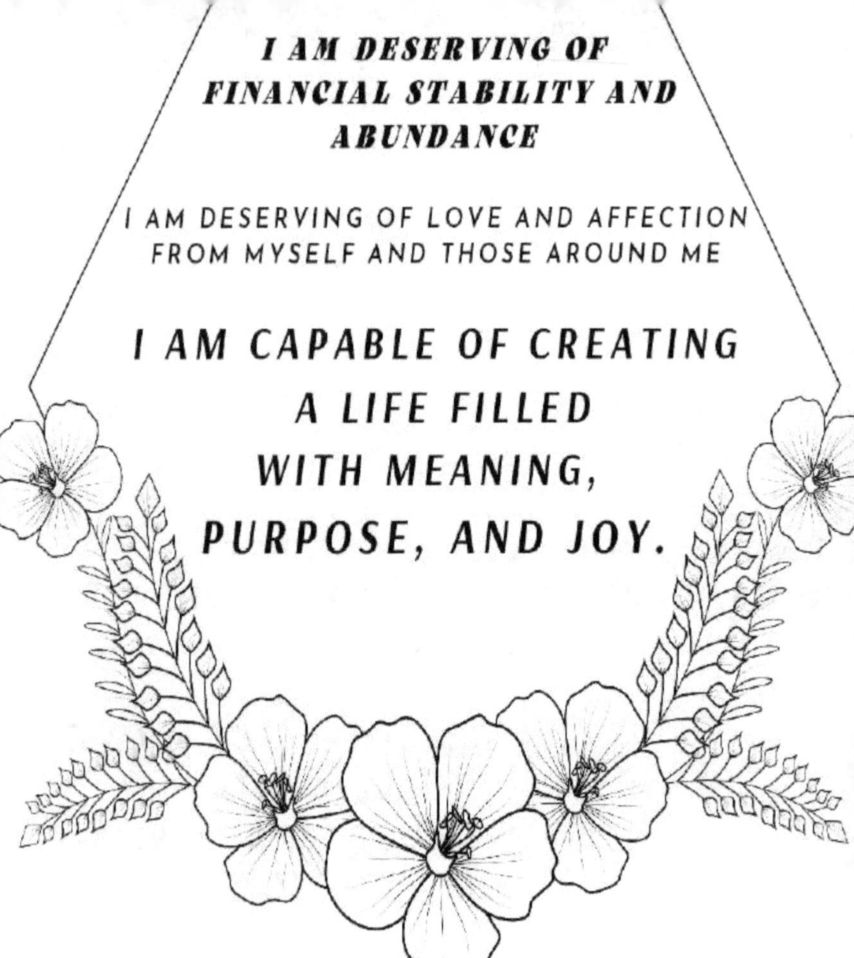

I AM DESERVING OF FINANCIAL STABILITY AND ABUNDANCE
I AM DESERVING OF LOVE AND AFFECTION FROM MYSELF AND THOSE AROUND ME
I AM CAPABLE OF CREATING A LIFE FILLED WITH MEANING, PURPOSE, AND JOY.
I AM PROUD OF MY RESILIENCE AND ABILITY TO BOUNCE BACK FROM SETBACKS
I AM CAPABLE OF SHOWING COMPASSION AND EMPATHY TOWARDS OTHERS

I AM LIVING MY BEST LIFE.

I AM CONFIDENT IN MY ABILITY TO PURSUE
MY PASSIONS AND MAKE THEM A
REALITY.

~ "*°•.~ "*°• I AM CAPABLE OF CREATING A POSITIVE
IMPACT ON THE WORLD AND LEAVING A
LEGACY OF COMPASSION AND KINDNESS •°*˜~.•°*˜~

I WILL NEVER ABANDON MYSELF

I am confident in my ability
to handle
stress and adversity with ease

THE OPPORTUNITIES TO LEARN AND GROW FROM MY MISTAKES. ♥

I am confident in my ability to trust my intuition and make wise decisions.

I am deserving of respect and kindness in all my interactions.

I AM CAPABLE OF FINDING PEACE AND TRANQUILITY IN ANY SITUATION.

I AM PROUD OF MYSELF FOR BEING TRUE TO WHO I AM AND LIVING AUTHENTICALLY.

I am confident in my ability to express myself creatively and pursue my passions.

I AM DESERVING OF FORGIVENESS AND COMPASSION TOWARDS MYSELF AND OTHERS.

I AM CONFIDENT IN MY ABILITY TO EXPRESS MYSELF CREATIVELY AND PURSUE MY PASSIONS.

I AM INTELLIGENT AND CAPABLE.

I AM CAPABLE OF OVERCOMING FEAR AND STEPPING OUTSIDE OF MY COMFORT ZONE.

I AM CONFIDENT IN MY ABILITY TO CULTIVATE POSITIVE AND HEALTHY HABITS.

I AM PROUD OF MY ACCOMPLISHMENTS, BIG AND SMALL.

AM CONFIDENT IN MY ABILITY TO COMMUNICATE EFFECTIVELY AND ASSERTIVELY

I AM GRATEFUL FOR THE EXPERIENCES THAT HAVE SHAPED ME INTO THE PERSON I AM TODAY.

I AM CAPABLE OF EMBRACING MY IMPERFECTIONS AND LOVING MYSELF UNCONDITIONALLY.

I AM DESERVING OF A LIFE FILLED WITH ADVENTURE AND EXPLORATION.

✦ I AM CAPABLE OF FINDING JOY AND BEAUTY IN THE WORLD AROUND ME.

I AM CONFIDENT IN MY ABILITY TO LEARN FROM MY MISTAKES AND USE THEM AS OPPORTUNITIES FOR GROWTH.

I AM CAPABLE OF CREATING A LIFE FILLED WITH PURPOSE, MEANING, AND FULFILLMENT.

I AM CONFIDENT IN MY ABILITY TO SET BOUNDARIES AND PRIORITIZE MY NEEDS.

I AM DESERVING OF LOVE AND ACCEPTANCE, JUST AS I AM.

•✥★I am grateful for my inner stren
and
resilience that carries me
through difficult
times.★✥•

I AM DESERVING OF SUPPORTIVE AND EMPOWERING RELATIONSHIPS THAT LIFT ME

I AM CAPABLE OF LIVING IN THE PRESENT
MOMENT AND FINDING JOY IN THE SIMPLE
THINGS.

I AM PROUD OF MY UNIQUE STRENGTHS AND
TALENTS THAT MAKE ME WHO I AM.

I AM DESERVING OF RESPECT, KINDNESS,
AND SUPPORT IN ALL MY RELATIONSHIPS.

I AM GRATEFUL FOR MY BODY AND ALL THAT IT
DOES TO SUPPORT ME.

I AM DESERVING OF UNCONDITIONAL LOVE
AND ACCEPTANCE FROM MYSELF AND
OTHERS.

I AM CAPABLE OF CREATING A POSITIVE
IMPACT ON THE WORLD AND LEAVING A
LASTING LEGACY.

I AM DESERVING OF A LIFE FILLED WITH
PASSION, PURPOSE, AND FULFILLMENT.

I AM CONFIDENT IN MY ABILITY TO SET AND
ACHIEVE MEANINGFUL GOALS.

I AM CAPABLE OF FINDING
BALANCE IN MY
LIFE AND PRIORITIZING MY
WELL-BEING.

I AM CONFIDENT IN MY ABILITY TO HANDLE
ANY CHALLENGE THAT COMES MY WAY

I AM GRATEFUL FOR THE
LOVE AND SUPPORT
OF THOSE AROUND ME.

I AM CONFIDENT IN MY ABILITY TO CREATE A
LIFE THAT BRINGS ME HAPPINESS AND
FULFILLMENT.

of happiness
and fulfillment in all
areas of my life

I am proud of my
unique perspective
and contributions to
the world.

I AM CAPABLE OF BUILDING HEALTHY AND
LOVING RELATIONSHIPS.

I AM CONFIDENT IN MY ABILITY TO
COMMUNICATE CLEARLY AND EFFECTIVELY.

I AM DESERVING OF SELF-CARE AND
PRIORITIZING MY OWN NEEDS.

I AM CAPABLE OF LIVING A LIFE FILLED WITH
PURPOSE AND MEANING.

I AM GRATEFUL FOR THE BEAUTY AND
WONDER OF THE WORLD AROUND ME.

I AM CONFIDENT IN MY ABILITY TO
OVERCOME OBSTACLES AND GROW STRONGER.

*I CHOOSE AUTHENTICITY OVER
PERFECTION.*

I am confident in my ability
to make a difference
in the lives of others.

≡★ *I am deserving of financial stability and success.* ★≡

I AM CAPABLE OF SHOWING COMPASSION
AND EMPATHY TOWARDS OTHERS.

I AM PROUD OF MY ACCOMPLISHMENTS AND
THE PROGRESS I'VE MADE.

I AM CONFIDENT IN MY ABILITY TO CREATE
POSITIVE CHANGE IN THE WORLD.

I AM DESERVING OF A LIFE FILLED WITH
ADVENTURE, EXCITEMENT, AND NEW
EXPERIENCES.

I AM CAPABLE OF LIVING IN ALIGNMENT WITH
MY VALUES AND BELIEFS.

I AM GRATEFUL FOR THE ABUNDANCE OF LOVE

Y LOVE FOR MYSELF IS
BOLD, FIERCE,
AND UNCONDITIONAL.

**AM DESERVING OF REST AND RELAXATION TO
RECHARGE AND REJUVENATE.**

I AM GRATEFUL FOR THE STRENGTH AND
COURAGE WITHIN ME.

AM CONFIDENT IN MY ABILITY TO CREATE A
LIFE OF MY OWN DESIGN.

I AM DESERVING OF SUCCESS AND
PROSPERITY IN ALL AREAS OF MY LIFE.

I AM CAPABLE OF MAKING POSITIVE
CHANGES IN MY LIFE TO ACHIEVE MY GOALS.

I AM PROUD OF THE PERSON I AM
BECOMING AND THE PROGRESS I HAVE
MADE.

I AM CAPABLE OF LIVING A LIFE OF
FULFILLMENT, PURPOSE, AND JOY

AM CONFIDENT IN MY ABILITY TO HANDLE
ANY CHALLENGES THAT COME MY WAY.

I AM DESERVING OF LOVE AND RESPECT
FROM MYSELF AND OTHERS.
(っ・◡・)っ ♥
I AM CAPABLE OF MANIFESTING
ABUNDANCE
AND PROSPERITY IN MY LIFE. ♥

I AM GRATEFUL FOR THE OPPORTUNITIES THAT
COME MY WAY TO LEARN AND GROW.

I AM CONFIDENT IN MY ABILITY TO LIVE
AUTHENTICALLY AND TRUE TO MYSELF.

I AM DESERVING OF A LIFE FILLED WITH LOVE, JOY, AND PEACE.

I AM CAPABLE OF ACHIEVING MY DREAMS AND CREATING A LIFE O
PURPOSE.

I AM BECOMING MORE CONFIDENT EACH DAY

I AM A CARING, COMPASSIONATE,
LOVING HUMAN BEING, AND I AM DOING THE BEST I CAN.
AND THAT IS ENOUGH.

I AM CONFIDENT
IN MY ABILITY TO
OVERCOME
ANY OBSTACLES AND
CHALLENGES
THAT COME MY WAY

I AM DESERVING OF A LIFE THAT IS FULFILLING,
REWARDING, AND SATISFYING.

I AM CAPABLE OF EXPRESSING MYSELF
CREATIVELY AND AUTHENTICALLY.

I AM GRATEFUL FOR MY HEALTH AND VITALITY
AND TAKE GOOD CARE OF MYSELF.

I AM CONFIDENT IN MY ABILITY TO BUILD
HEALTHY RELATIONSHIPS WITH OTHERS.

I AM DESERVING OF SUCCESS AND
RECOGNITION FOR MY HARD WORK AND
ACHIEVEMENTS.

I AM CAPABLE OF CREATING A LIFE OF MY
OWN DESIGN THAT BRINGS ME HAPPINESS,
PEACE, AND FULFILLMENT.

I AM GRATEFUL FOR THE OPPORTUNITIES TO LEARN AND GROW EACH DAY.

I AM CONFIDENT IN MY ABILITY TO ACHIEVE MY GOALS AND DREAMS.

I AM DESERVING OF RESPECT AND KINDNESS FROM MYSELF AND OTHERS.

I AM CAPABLE OF EMBRACING CHANGE AND ADAPTING TO NEW SITUATIONS.

I AM PROUD OF MY UNIQUE TALENTS AND ABILITIES.

I AM CONFIDENT IN MY ABILITY TO MAKE A POSITIVE IMPACT ON THE WORLD.

I AM DESERVING OF LOVE AND COMPASSION FROM MYSELF AND OTHERS.

I AM CAPABLE OF CREATING A LIFE FILLED WITH LOVE, JOY, AND ABUNDANCE.

I AM GRATEFUL FOR THE BEAUTY AND WONDER OF THE NATURAL WORLD.

I AM CONFIDENT IN MY ABILITY TO MAKE THE MOST OF EACH DAY.

I AM CAPABLE OF OVERCOMING MY FEARS AND DOUBTS.

I AM PROUD OF THE PERSON I AM AND THE PERSON I AM BECOMING

I AM DESERVING OF SELF-CARE AND TAKING TIME TO RECHARGE.

I AM CAPABLE OF ACHIEVING A BALANCE BETWEEN WORK AND PLAY.

I AM GRATEFUL FOR THE LOVE AND SUPPORT OF MY FAMILY AND FRIENDS.

I AM CONFIDENT IN MY ABILITY TO CREATE HEALTHY BOUNDARIES AND RELATIONSHIPS.

I AM CONFIDENT IN MY ABILITY TO EXPRESS MYSELF AUTHENTICALLY.

I AM DESERVING OF FORGIVENESS AND
COMPASSION FOR MYSELF AND OTHERS.

**I AM CAPABLE OF ACHIEVING MY DREAMS
AND CREATING A LIFE OF JOY AND PURPOSE.**

I AM GRATEFUL FOR THE PRESENT MOMENT
AND ALL THAT IT BRINGS.

*I AM CONFIDENT IN MY ABILITY TO MAKE
THE MOST OF MY TIME AND OPPORTUNITIES.*

I AM DESERVING OF HAPPINESS AND
FULFILLMENT IN ALL AREAS OF MY
LIFE.

**I AM CAPABLE OF ACHIEVING A STATE OF
INNER PEACE AND CALM.**

*I AM CONFIDENT IN MY ABILITY TO LEARN
FROM MY MISTAKES AND GROW*

I AM DESERVING OF SELF-LOVE AND
ACCEPTANCE.

I AM PROUD OF MY ACCOMPLISHMENTS AND
THE PROGRESS I HAVE MADE

I AM CAPABLE OF ACHIEVING SUCCESS AND PROSPERITY IN MY CAREER

I AM GRATEFUL FOR THE ABUNDANCE OF OPPORTUNITIES AND BLESSINGS IN MY LIFE.

I AM CONFIDENT IN MY ABILITY TO HANDLE ANY CHALLENGES THAT COME MY WAY WITH GRACE AND EASE.

I AM DESERVING OF A LIFE THAT IS ALIGNED WITH MY VALUES AND BELIEFS.

I AM CAPABLE OF CREATING MEANINGFUL AND FULFILLING RELATIONSHIPS WITH OTHERS

I AM PROUD OF MY RESILIENCE AND ABILITY TO BOUNCE BACK FROM SETBACKS

I AM DESERVING OF RESPECT AND DIGNITY IN ALL AREAS OF MY LIFE.

I AM CAPABLE OF FINDING SOLUTIONS TO ANY PROBLEMS I ENCOUNTER.

I AM CONFIDENT IN MY ABILITY TO MAKE POSITIVE CONTRIBUTIONS TO THE WORLD.

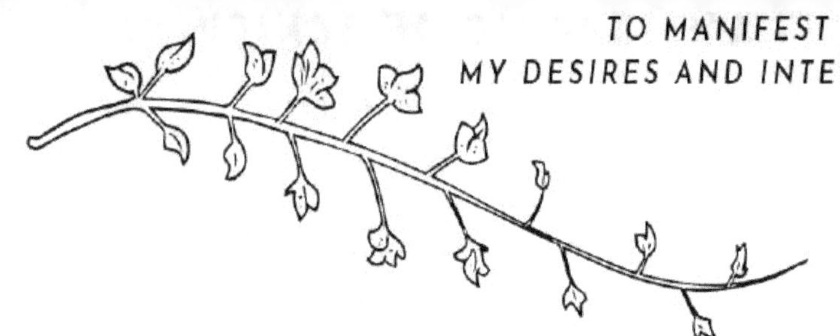

TO MANIFEST
MY DESIRES AND INTENTIONS.

I AM GRATEFUL FOR MY INNER STRENGTH AND
COURAGE.

I AM DESERVING OF A LIFE THAT IS FREE FROM
STRESS AND NEGATIVITY.

I AM CAPABLE OF ACHIEVING MY HIGHEST
POTENTIAL AND LIVING A LIFE OF PURPOSE
AND PASSION

**I AM DESERVING OF ALL THE SUCCESS AND
HAPPINESS THAT COMES MY WAY.**

**I AM CAPABLE OF CREATING A LIFE THAT IS
AUTHENTIC AND ALIGNED WITH MY
PURPOSE.**

I AM PROUD OF THE PROGRESS I HAVE MADE
AND THE PERSON I AM BECOMING.

I AM GRATEFUL FOR THE ABUNDANCE OF LOVE IN MY LIFE.
I AM CONFIDENT IN MY ABILITY TO CREATE A POSITIVE IMPACT ON THE WORLD AROUND ME.
I AM DESERVING OF ALL THE GOOD THAT COMES MY WAY.
I AM CAPABLE OF FINDING JOY IN THE SIMPLEST OF THINGS.
I AM PROUD OF THE PERSON I AM BECOMING, AND I EMBRACE ALL ASPECTS OF MYSELF.
I AM CONFIDENT IN MY ABILITY TO COMMUNICATE MY THOUGHTS AND FEELINGS EFFECTIVELY.
I AM DESERVING OF A LIFE FILLED WITH LAUGHTER, JOY, AND ADVENTURE.
I AM CAPABLE OF OVERCOMING ANY OBSTACLE THAT COMES MY WAY.
I AM GRATEFUL FOR THE BEAUTY AND MAGIC OF THE WORLD AROUND ME.
I AM CONFIDENT IN MY ABILITY TO MAKE DECISIONS THAT SERVE MY HIGHEST GOOD.

SUCCESS AND ABUNDANCE ARE MY BIRTHRIGHTS.

I AM GRATEFUL FOR MY BODY AND ALL THAT IT CAN DO.

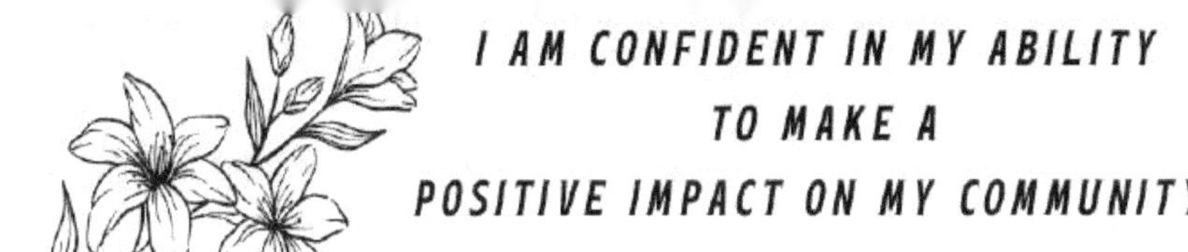

I AM CONFIDENT IN MY ABILITY
TO MAKE A
POSITIVE IMPACT ON MY COMMUNITY.

I AM DESERVING OF LOVE AND RESPECT
FROM MYSELF AND OTHERS.

I AM CAPABLE OF FINDING SOLUTIONS TO ANY
CHALLENGE THAT COMES MY WAY.

I AM PROUD OF MY UNIQUE QUALITIES AND
THE GIFTS I HAVE TO OFFER THE WORLD

*I AM CONFIDENT IN MY ABILITY TO NAVIGATE
CHANGE AND UNCERTAINTY WITH EASE.*

AM DESERVING OF A LIFE THAT IS FILLED
WITH ABUNDANCE AND PROSPERITY.

I AM CAPABLE OF CREATING A LIFE THAT IS
ALIGNED WITH MY VALUES AND BELIEFS.

I AM GRATEFUL FOR THE OPPORTUNITY TO
LEARN AND GROW EVERY DAY.

I AM CONFIDENT IN MY ABILITY TO CONNECT
WITH OTHERS ON A DEEP AND MEANINGFUL
LEVEL

I AM DESERVING OF A LIFE
THAT IS FREE FROM
WORRY AND ANXIETY.

I AM CAPABLE OF ACHIEVING MY DREAMS
AND LIVING A LIFE OF PURPOSE.

I AM PROUD OF MY RESILIENCE AND
STRENGTH IN THE FACE OF ADVERSITY.

I AM CONFIDENT IN MY ABILITY TO MAKE
EMPOWERED DECISIONS THAT SERVE MY
HIGHEST GOOD.

I AM DESERVING OF A LIFE THAT IS FILLED
WITH JOY, PASSION, AND FULFILLMENT.

I AM CAPABLE OF CREATING A LIFE THAT IS
FULL OF MEANING AND PURPOSE.

I AM GRATEFUL FOR THE BLESSINGS AND
OPPORTUNITIES IN MY LIFE.

I AM CONFIDENT IN MY ABILITY TO LIVE
AUTHENTICALLY AND TRUE TO MYSELF.

I AM DESERVING OF A LIFE THAT IS FILLED
WITH PEACE, BALANCE, AND HARMONY.

I AM CAPABLE OF CREATING A LIFE THAT IS
FILLED WITH BEAUTY, WONDER, AND MAGIC

I AM PROUD OF MYSELF FOR ALL THE PROGRESS I
HAVE MADE AND ALL THE CHALLENGES I HAVE
OVERCOME

I AM CONFIDENT IN MY ABILITY TO CREATE A LIFE
THAT IS ALIGNED WITH MY PASSIONS AND
PURPOSE.

I AM GRATEFUL FOR THE PRESENT MOMENT AND
ALL THAT IT OFFERS ME.

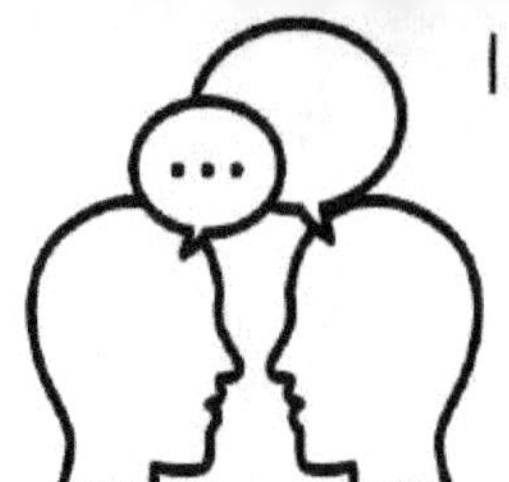

I am confident in my ability to communicate
my needs and wants effectively.

I AM DESERVING OF A LIFE THAT
IS FREE FROM
COMPARISON AND SELF-DOUBT.

I AM CAPABLE OF LOVING AND ACCEPTING
MYSELF UNCONDITIONALLY.

I AM PROUD OF MY UNIQUE QUALITIES AND
THE GIFTS THAT I BRING TO THE WORLD.

I AM CONFIDENT IN MY ABILITY TO HANDLE
ANY CHALLENGE THAT COMES MY WAY.

I AM DESERVING OF A LIFE THAT IS FILLED
WITH PURPOSE AND PASSION.

I AM CAPABLE OF CREATING A LIFE THAT IS IN
ALIGNMENT WITH MY TRUE SELF.

I AM GRATEFUL FOR THE OPPORTUNITIES THAT
COME MY WAY, AND I EMBRACE THEM WITH
AN OPEN HEART AND MIND.

I AM CONFIDENT IN MY ABILITY TO NAVIGATE
CHANGE AND ADAPT TO NEW SITUATIONS.

I AM DESERVING OF A LIFE THAT IS FILLED
WITH LOVE, JOY, AND PEACE.

I AM CAPABLE OF CREATING A LIFE THAT IS
ABUNDANT IN ALL AREAS OF MY LIFE.

I am grateful for my strengths and weaknesses, as they make me unique.

I AM GRATEFUL FOR MY STRENGTHS AND WEAKNESSES, AS THEY MAKE ME UNIQUE.

I AM CONFIDENT IN MY ABILITY TO CREATE A LIFE THAT IS FILLED WITH POSITIVITY AND LIGHT.

I AM DESERVING OF RESPECT AND LOVE FROM MYSELF AND OTHERS.

I AM CAPABLE OF FINDING MY TRUE PURPOSE AND FULFILLING MY LIFE'S MISSION.

I AM PROUD OF ALL THE ACHIEVEMENTS AND ACCOMPLISHMENTS IN MY LIFE.

I AM CONFIDENT IN MY ABILITY TO MAKE A DIFFERENCE IN THE WORLD.

I AM DESERVING OF A LIFE THAT IS FILLED WITH ABUNDANCE, PROSPERITY, AND SUCCESS.

I AM CAPABLE OF ACHIEVING ANYTHING THAT I SET MY MIND TO.
I AM GRATEFUL FOR THE OPPORTUNITIES TO LEARN AND GROW THAT COME MY WAY.

I AM CONFIDENT IN MY ABILITY TO CONNECT

I AM DESERVING OF A LIFE
THAT IS FREE FROM
JUDGMENT AND CRITICISM.

I AM CAPABLE OF LOVING AND ACCEPTING
MYSELF UNCONDITIONALLY.

I AM PROUD OF MY UNIQUE PERSPECTIVE
AND THE WAY I SEE THE WORLD.

I AM CONFIDENT IN MY ABILITY TO
OVERCOME ANY OBSTACLE IN MY PATH.

I AM DESERVING OF A LIFE THAT IS FILLED
WITH BALANCE, HARMONY, AND PEACE.

I AM CAPABLE OF CREATING A LIFE THAT IS IN
ALIGNMENT WITH MY HIGHEST SELF.

I AM GRATEFUL FOR THE BEAUTY AND
WONDER THAT EXISTS IN THE WORLD AROUND
ME.

I AM CONFIDENT IN MY ABILITY TO LEAD AND
INSPIRE OTHERS.

I AM DESERVING OF A LIFE THAT IS FILLED
WITH LOVE, LAUGHTER, AND HAPPINESS.

I AM CAPABLE OF CREATING A LIFE THAT IS
FULL OF PURPOSE, MEANING, AND

I AM GRATEFUL FOR THE OPPORTUNITIES THAT
LIFE PRESENTS ME WITH.

I AM CONFIDENT IN MY ABILITY TO LEARN
AND GROW FROM EVERY EXPERIENCE.

I AM DESERVING OF A LIFE THAT IS FILLED
WITH SELF-LOVE AND SELF-ACCEPTANCE.

I AM CAPABLE OF ACHIEVING MY GOALS AND
FULFILLING MY DREAMS.

I AM PROUD OF MY ACCOMPLISHMENTS AND
CELEBRATE MY SUCCESSES.

I AM CONFIDENT IN MY ABILITY TO HANDLE
WHATEVER CHALLENGES COME MY WAY.

I AM DESERVING OF A LIFE THAT IS FILLED
WITH ABUNDANCE AND PROSPERITY.

I AM CAPABLE OF LIVING IN THE PRESENT
MOMENT AND ENJOYING EVERY MINUTE OF
IT.

I AM GRATEFUL FOR THE PEOPLE IN MY LIFE
WHO SUPPORT AND INSPIRE ME.

I AM CONFIDENT IN MY ABILITY TO CREATE A
LIFE THAT IS ALIGNED WITH MY VALUES AND

*THAT IS FILLED
WITH JOY AND HAPPINESS.*

I AM CAPABLE OF MAKING A DIFFERENCE IN
THE LIVES OF OTHERS.

I AM PROUD OF MY UNIQUE TALENTS AND
ABILITIES.

I AM CONFIDENT IN MY ABILITY TO MAKE
POSITIVE CHANGES IN THE WORLD.

I AM DESERVING OF A LIFE THAT IS FILLED
WITH MEANING AND PURPOSE.

I AM CAPABLE OF CREATING A LIFE THAT IS
AUTHENTIC AND TRUE TO WHO I AM.

I AM GRATEFUL FOR MY INNER STRENGTH AND
RESILIENCE.

I AM CONFIDENT IN MY ABILITY TO
OVERCOME ANY OBSTACLE.

I AM DESERVING OF A LIFE THAT IS FILLED
WITH BEAUTY AND WONDER.

I AM CAPABLE OF CREATING A LIFE THAT IS
FULL OF LOVE, LIGHT, AND HAPPINESS.

I AM GRATEFUL FOR THE
LOVE AND KINDNESS I
RECEIVE FROM OTHERS.

I AM CONFIDENT IN MY ABILITY TO TRUST MY
INTUITION AND MAKE WISE DECISIONS.

I AM DESERVING OF A LIFE THAT IS FILLED
WITH PEACE AND HARMONY.

I AM CAPABLE OF ACHIEVING BALANCE IN ALL
AREAS OF MY LIFE.

I AM PROUD OF MY UNIQUE PERSONALITY
AND EMBRACE MY INDIVIDUALITY.

I AM CONFIDENT IN MY ABILITY TO LEARN
AND GROW FROM MY MISTAKES.

I AM DESERVING OF A LIFE THAT IS FILLED
WITH RESPECT AND APPRECIATION.

I AM CAPABLE OF CREATING HEALTHY AND
LOVING RELATIONSHIPS WITH OTHERS.

I AM GRATEFUL FOR THE BEAUTY THAT
SURROUNDS ME IN THE WORLD.

I AM CONFIDENT IN MY ABILITY TO FOLLOW
MY HEART AND PURSUE MY PASSIONS.

I AM DESERVING OF A LIFE
THAT IS FILLED
WITH SUCCESS AND PROSPERITY.

I AM CAPABLE OF OVERCOMING
ANY FEAR OR
DOUBT THAT ARISES WITHIN ME.

I AM PROUD OF MY JOURNEY AND ALL THAT I HAVE ACCOMPLISHED.

I AM CONFIDENT IN MY ABILITY TO HANDLE
ANY CHALLENGE THAT COMES MY WAY.

I AM DESERVING OF A LIFE THAT IS FILLED
WITH HOPE AND OPTIMISM.

I AM CAPABLE OF CREATING A LIFE THAT IS I
ALIGNMENT WITH MY SOUL'S PURPOSE.

I AM CONFIDENT IN MY ABILITY TO MAKE A
POSITIVE IMPACT ON THE WORLD.

I AM DESERVING OF A LIFE THAT IS FILLED
WITH ADVENTURE AND EXPLORATION.

I AM GRATEFUL FOR THE EXPERIENCES THAT
HAVE SHAPED ME INTO THE PERSON I AM
TODAY.

*A LIFE THAT IS
FILLED WITH JOY AND
FULFILLMENT.*

I AM GRATEFUL FOR THE ABUNDANCE OF
OPPORTUNITIES THAT COME MY WAY.

I AM CONFIDENT IN MY ABILITY TO HANDLE
CHANGE AND ADAPT TO NEW SITUATIONS.
I AM DESERVING OF A LIFE THAT IS FILLED
WITH LAUGHTER AND HAPPINESS.

I AM CAPABLE OF CREATING HEALTHY
BOUNDARIES AND RESPECTING MY OWN
NEEDS.

I AM PROUD OF MY ACCOMPLISHMENTS AND
CELEBRATE MY ACHIEVEMENTS.

I AM CONFIDENT IN MY ABILITY TO ATTRACT
POSITIVE EXPERIENCES INTO MY LIFE.

I AM DESERVING OF A LIFE THAT IS FILLED
WITH LOVE AND COMPASSION.

I AM CAPABLE OF ACHIEVING MY GOALS AND
FULFILLING MY DREAMS.

I AM GRATEFUL FOR THE STRENGTH AND
RESILIENCE I POSSESS.

I AM CONFIDENT IN MY ABILITY TO
OVERCOME ANY OBSTACLE THAT COMES MY
WAY.

I AM DESERVING OF A LIFE
THAT IS FILLED
WITH PURPOSE AND FULFILLMENT.

I AM PROUD OF THE PERSON I AM
BECOMING AND EMBRACE MY JOURNEY.

I AM CAPABLE OF CREATING A LIFE THAT IS
ALIGNED WITH MY VALUES AND BELIEFS.

I AM CONFIDENT IN MY ABILITY TO MAKE A
POSITIVE IMPACT IN THE WORLD.

I AM DESERVING OF A LIFE THAT IS FILLED
WITH ABUNDANCE AND PROSPERITY.

I AM CAPABLE OF CREATING A LIFE THAT IS
FILLED WITH GRATITUDE AND APPRECIATION.

I AM GRATEFUL FOR THE SUPPORT AND LOVE I
RECEIVE FROM THOSE AROUND ME.

I AM CONFIDENT IN MY ABILITY TO TRUST
MYSELF AND MY INTUITION

I AM DESERVING OF A LIFE THAT IS FILLED
WITH PEACE AND CONTENTMENT.

I AM GRATEFUL FOR MY INNER STRENGTH AND
RESILIENCE.

I AM CAPABLE OF CREATING A LIFE THAT IS
FILLED WITH PURPOSE, PASSION, AND JOY.

I AM CONFIDENT IN MY ABILITY TO
OVERCOME ANY CHALLENGE OR
OBSTACLE
THAT COMES MY WAY.

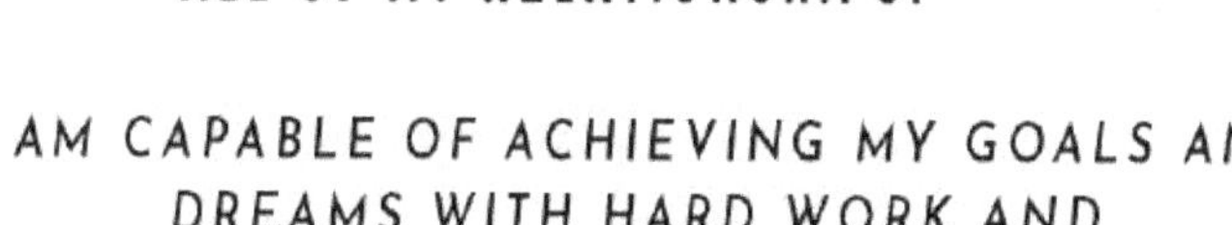

**AM DESERVING OF LOVE AND RESPECT IN
ALL OF MY RELATIONSHIPS.**

AM CAPABLE OF ACHIEVING MY GOALS AND
DREAMS WITH HARD WORK AND
DETERMINATION.

I AM PROUD OF WHO I AM AND ALL THAT I
HAVE ACCOMPLISHED.

I AM CONFIDENT IN MY ABILITY TO MAKE
DECISIONS THAT ALIGN WITH MY VALUES AND
BELIEFS.

I AM DESERVING OF A LIFE THAT IS FILLED
WITH ABUNDANCE AND PROSPERITY.

I AM CAPABLE OF CREATING A POSITIVE AND
LOVING ENVIRONMENT FOR MYSELF AND
THOSE AROUND ME.

I AM GRATEFUL FOR THE LESSONS I HAVE
LEARNED FROM MY PAST EXPERIENCES.

I AM CONFIDENT IN MY ABILITY TO LEARN,
GROW, AND EVOLVE AS A PERSON.

I AM PROUD OF MY UNIQUE TALENTS AND GIFTS, AND I SHARE THEM WITH THE WORLD.

I AM CONFIDENT IN MY ABILITY TO PURSUE MY PASSIONS AND LIVE A FULFILLING LIFE.

I AM DESERVING OF SELF-LOVE AND ACCEPTANCE, JUST AS I AM.

I AM CAPABLE OF CREATING A LIFE THAT IS FILLED WITH PURPOSE AND MEANING.

I AM GRATEFUL FOR THE SUPPORT AND ENCOURAGEMENT I RECEIVE FROM OTHERS. I AM CONFIDENT IN MY ABILITY TO MANIFEST MY DESIRES AND CREATE THE LIFE I WANT.

I AM DESERVING OF A LIFE THAT IS FILLED WITH POSITIVITY AND OPTIMISM.

I AM CAPABLE OF ACHIEVING ANYTHING I SET MY MIND TO AND REALIZING MY FULL
POTENTIAL.

MY SUPPORTIVE AND
LOVING RELATIONSHIPS

I AM DESERVING OF SELF-CARE AND
PRIORITIZE IT IN MY LIFE.

I AM CONFIDENT IN
MY ABILITIES AND TRUST
IN MY OWN JUDGEMENT.

M CAPABLE OF LEARNING AND GROWING
FROM EVERY EXPERIENCE.

I AM PROUD OF MY RESILIENCE AND ABILITY
TO BOUNCE BACK FROM CHALLENGES.

AM GRATEFUL FOR THE OPPORTUNITIES THAT
ALLOW ME TO LEARN AND GROW.

I AM DESERVING OF ABUNDANCE AND
PROSPERITY IN ALL AREAS OF MY LIFE.

**I AM CONFIDENT IN MY ABILITY TO MAKE
POSITIVE CHANGES IN MY LIFE.**

I AM EMPOWERED TO CREATE MY OWN
HAPPINESS AND TAKE CONTROL OF MY LIFE.

*I AM GRATEFUL FOR THE JOURNEY OF
SELF DISCOVERY AND PERSONAL GROWTH THAT*

IN MY OWN SKIN AND
LOVE MYSELF
UNCONDITIONALLY.

I TRUST THE UNIVERSE TO GUIDE ME
TOWARDS MY HIGHEST GOOD.

I AM WORTHY OF FORGIVENESS AND CHOOSE
TO RELEASE ANY NEGATIVITY FROM MY PAST.

I AM CONFIDENT IN MY ABILITY TO SET
BOUNDARIES THAT PROTECT MY WELL-BEING.
I AM DESERVING OF A FULFILLING AND
MEANINGFUL LIFE.

I AM CAPABLE OF ACHIEVING MY DREAMS
AND MAKING THEM A REALITY.

I AM EMPOWERED TO FOLLOW MY PASSIONS
AND LIVE A LIFE THAT IS TRUE TO ME.

I AM PROUD OF MY RESILIENCE AND ABILITY
TO OVERCOME CHALLENGES.

I AM GRATEFUL FOR MY UNIQUE TALENTS AND
USE THEM TO MAKE A POSITIVE IMPACT.

I AM CONFIDENT IN MY ABILITY TO LOVE AND
BE LOVED.

I AM WORTH OF LOVE AND RESPECT, JUST AS I AM.

I AM CONFIDENT IN MY ABILITY TO MAKE WISE DECISIONS.
I AM GRATEFUL FOR ALL THE OPPORTUNITIES THAT COME MY WAY.
I AM DESERVING OF SUCCESS AND ACHIEVEMENT IN ALL AREAS OF MY LIFE.
I AM CAPABLE OF OVERCOMING ANY OBSTACLE THAT STANDS IN MY WAY.
I AM EMPOWERED TO EXPRESS MYSELF AND MY NEEDS IN A HEALTHY AND POSITIVE WAY.
I AM WORTHY OF FORGIVENESS AND COMPASSION, BOTH FOR MYSELF AND OTHERS.
I AM CONFIDENT IN MY ABILITY TO LEARN AND GROW FROM MY MISTAKES.
I AM GRATEFUL FOR THE BEAUTY AND WONDER OF THE WORLD AROUND ME.
I AM DESERVING OF HAPPINESS AND FULFILLMENT IN ALL ASPECTS OF MY LIFE.

I AM CAPABLE OF CREATING MEANINGFUL
AND LASTING CONNECTIONS WITH
OTHERS.

I AM EMPOWERED TO EMBRACE MY
AUTHENTIC SELF AND LIVE MY TRUTH.

I AM WORTHY OF TAKING UP SPACE AND
BEING SEEN AND HEARD.

I AM CAPABLE OF ACHIEVING MY DREAMS
AND REACHING MY GOALS.

I AM EMPOWERED TO SPEAK MY TRUTH AND
ADVOCATE FOR MYSELF AND OTHERS.

I AM WORTHY OF EXPERIENCING PLEASURE
AND JOY IN MY LIFE.

I AM CONFIDENT IN MY ABILITY TO CREATE A
LIFE THAT I LOVE

I AM GRATEFUL FOR THE ABUNDANCE AND
BLESSINGS IN MY LIFE.

I AM DESERVING OF LOVE AND CARE FROM
THOSE AROUND ME.

I AM CAPABLE OF ACHIEVING
GREATNESS AND
FULFILLING
MY POTENTIAL.

MY LIFE IS A MIRACLE,
AND I BELONG HERE.

*I AM GRATEFUL FOR MY INNER STRENGTH
AND RESILIENCE.*

*I AM DESERVING OF RESPECT AND EQUAL
TREATMENT IN ALL AREAS OF MY LIFE.*

*I AM EMPOWERED TO MAKE CHOICES THAT
ALIGN WITH MY VALUES AND GOALS.*

*I AM WORTHY OF SELF-LOVE AND SELF-CARE,
AND I PRIORITIZE MY WELL-BEING.*

I AM GRATEFUL FOR THE SUPPORT AND
ENCOURAGEMENT OF THOSE WHO BELIEVE IN
ME.
I AM DESERVING OF SUCCESS AND
RECOGNITION FOR MY HARD WORK AND
ACHIEVEMENTS.

I AM CONFIDENT IN MY ABILITY TO LEARN AND
GROW FROM CHALLENGES AND SETBACKS.

WOMEN ARE VALUABLE CONTRIBUTORS TO SOCIETY AND SHOULD BE RECOGNIZED FOR THEIR CONTRIBUTIONS

I AM DESERVING OF LOVE AND AFFECTION, AND I GIVE AND RECEIVE IT FREELY.

I AM CAPABLE OF ACHIEVING BALANCE AND HARMONY IN ALL AREAS OF MY LIFE.

I AM EMPOWERED TO SET HEALTHY BOUNDARIES AND PROTECT MY OWN WELL BEING.

I AM WORTHY OF FINANCIAL STABILITY AND ABUNDANCE.

I AM CONFIDENT IN MY ABILITY TO MANIFEST MY DREAMS AND DESIRES.

I AM GRATEFUL FOR THE OPPORTUNITIES AND EXPERIENCES THAT HAVE SHAPED ME INTO WHO I AM.

I AM DESERVING OF RESPECT AND ADMIRATION FOR THE UNIQUE QUALITIES AND STRENGTHS THAT I POSSESS.

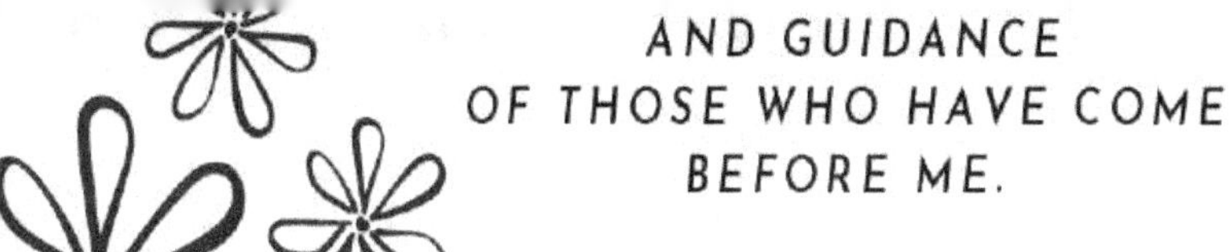

AND GUIDANCE
OF THOSE WHO HAVE COME
BEFORE ME.

I AM EMPOWERED TO SPEAK MY TRUTH AND
STAND UP FOR WHAT I BELIEVE IN.

I AM DESERVING OF FORGIVENESS AND RELEASE
FROM PAST MISTAKES OR REGRETS.

AM WORTHY OF LOVE AND RESPECT FROM THOSE
IN MY PERSONAL AND PROFESSIONAL
RELATIONSHIPS.

I AM CAPABLE OF ACHIEVING BALANCE BETWEEN
MY PERSONAL AND PROFESSIONAL LIFE.

I AM CONFIDENT IN MY ABILITY TO HANDLE ANY
CHALLENGES THAT COME MY WAY.

I AM GRATEFUL FOR THE BEAUTY
AND ABUNDANCE
OF NATURE AND THE WORLD AROUND ME.

I AM DESERVING OF SUPPORT AND
ENCOURAGEMENT IN MY PERSONAL AND
PROFESSIONAL PURSUITS

I AM EMPOWERED TO MAKE
POSITIVE CHANGES
IN MY LIFE AND THE LIVES
OF THOSE AROUND ME.

I AM GRATEFUL FOR THE ABUNDANCE OF OPPORTUNITIES AND BLESSINGS IN MY LIFE

I AM EMPOWERED TO HAVE THE THINGS I SEEK.

I AM WORTHY OF A LIFE FILLED WITH PEACE, HARMONY, AND BALANCE.

I AM CAPABLE OF PRACTICING SELF COMPASSION AND FORGIVENESS TOWARDS MYSELF.

I AM CONFIDENT IN MY ABILITY TO HANDLE CHANGE AND ADAPT TO NEW CIRCUMSTANCES.

I AM EMPOWERED TO USE MY VOICE TO ADVOCATE FOR CAUSES THAT MATTER TO ME.

I AM CONFIDENT IN MY ABILITY TO CREATE AND MAINTAIN A LIFE THAT ALIGNS WITH MY VALUES.

I AM DESERVING OF A LIFE FILLED WITH LOVE HAPPINESS, AND FULFILLMENT.

I AM GRATEFUL FOR MY INNER STRENGTH ANDRESILIENCE.

I AM WORTHY OF FORGIVENESS, BOTH FROM OTHERS AND FROM MYSELF.

I AM CONFIDENT IN MY ABILITY TO FOLLOW MY DREAMS AND PASSIONS.

I AM CAPABLE OF LIVING A LIFE OF AUTHENTICITY AND PURPOSE, AND INSPIRE OTHERS TO DO THE SAME.

I AM CAPABLE OF EMBRACING CHANGE AND SEEING IT AS AN OPPORTUNITY FOR GROWTH AND TRANSFORMATION.

I TRUST IN MY INTUITION AND FOLLOW IT WITH COURAGE AND TRUST.

I AM WORTHY OF TAKING TIME FOR MYSELF AND PRIORITIZING MY OWN NEEDS AND DESIRES

I FULLY LOVE AND EMBRACE WHO I AM NOW, EVEN AS I CONTINUE TO GROW.

I AM CONFIDENT IN MY ABILITY TO HANDLE ANY CHALLENGE THAT COMES MY WAY WITH GRACE AND STRENGTH.

I RELEASE ANYTHING THAT DOESN'T SUPPORT MY HIGHEST GOOD.

I AM DESERVING OF HAPPINESS AND JOY IN EVERY AREA OF MY LIFE.

I AM CAPABLE OF CREATING HEALTHY BOUNDARIES AND SAYING NO WHEN NECESSARY.

I AM PROUD OF MY INNER AND OUTER BEAUTY, AND EMBRACE THEM BOTH WITH LOVE AND ACCEPTANCE.

I TRUST IN THE JOURNEY OF MY LIFE, KNOWING THAT EVERYTHING HAPPENS FOR A REASON AND FOR MY HIGHEST GOOD.

I AM DESERVING OF POSITIVE AND SUPPORTIVE RELATIONSHIPS THAT UPLIFT AND INSPIRE ME.

I AM PROUD OF MY UNIQUENESS AND INDIVIDUALITY.

I TRUST IN MY ABILITY TO MAKE A POSITIVE IMPACT ON THE WORLD.

I AM WORTHY OF RECEIVING LOVE AND ATTENTION FROM THOSE AROUND ME

I AM CONFIDENT IN MY ABILITY TO EXPRESS MY TRUE FEELINGS AND EMOTIONS.

I AM DESERVING OF HAPPINESS AND FULFILLMENT IN ALL AREAS OF MY LIFE.

I AM CAPABLE OF CREATING A LIFE THAT ALIGNS WITH MY VALUES AND BELIEFS.

I AM GRATEFUL FOR THE OPPORTUNITIES THAT COME MY WAY AND EMBRACE THEM WITH ENTHUSIASM.

I AM CONFIDENT IN MY ABILITY TO
MANIFEST MY DREAMS AND DESIRES
INTO REALITY.

I AM CAPABLE OF LETTING GO
OF ANY NEGATIVE
SELF-TALK OR LIMITING
BELIEFS THAT HOLD ME BACK.

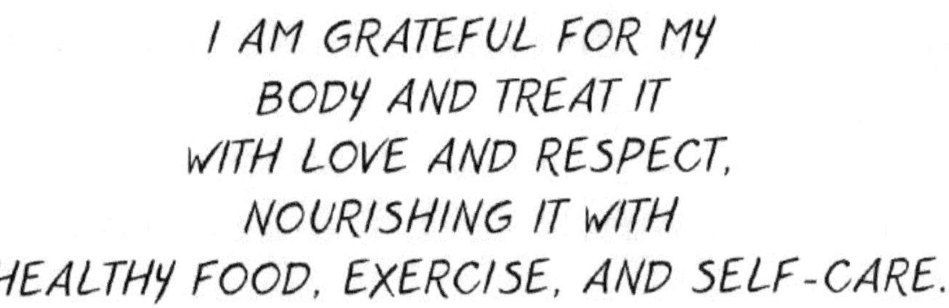

*I AM GRATEFUL FOR MY
BODY AND TREAT IT
WITH LOVE AND RESPECT,
NOURISHING IT WITH
HEALTHY FOOD, EXERCISE, AND SELF-CARE.*

I AM WORTHY OF FORGIVENESS AND
RELEASE ANY GUILT OR SHAME FROM
PAST MISTAKES.

*I AM PROUD OF THE PERSON I AM AND THE PERSON I AM
BECOMING.*

I AM PROUD OF MY ACHIEVEMENTS
AND CELEBRATE THEM WITH JOY AND
GRATITUDE.

*I TRUST IN MY ABILITY
TO HANDLE ANY CHALLENGE
THAT COMES MY WAY
WITH GRACE AND STRENGTH.*

I TRUST IN MY INTUITION AND FOLLOW IT WITH CONFIDENCE.

**I AM CONFIDENT IN MY ABILITY TO
LEARN AND GROW FROM MY EXPERIENCES.**

I AM CAPABLE OF ACHIEVING MY GOALS
AND DREAMS, NO MATTER HOW BIG OR
SMALL THEY MAY BE.

I AM WORTHY OF TAKING CARE OF MYSELF
AND PRIORITIZING MY OWN WELL-BEING.

I AM CONFIDENT IN MY ABILITY
TO SPEAK MY TRUTH AND
STAND UP FOR MYSELF AND OTHERS.

I AM DESERVING OF FINANCIAL ABUNDANCE
AND SUCCESS IN MY CAREER OR BUSINESS.

AM CAPABLE OF ACHIEVING BALANCE AND
HARMONY IN ALL ASPECTS OF MY LIFE.

I AM CAPABLE OF CULTIVATING
A POSITIVE MINDSET, AND ATTRACT POSITIVE
EXPERIENCES AND OPPORTUNITIES INTO MY

I AM PROUD OF MY RESILIENCE
AND ABILITY TO BOUNCE
BACK FROM ANY SETBACKS
OR CHALLENGES.

I AM GRATEFUL FOR THE LESSONS
AND GROWTH THAT COME FROM
DIFFICULT EXPERIENCES.

I AM GRATEFUL FOR
MY UNIQUE PERSPECTIVE
AND EXPERIENCES THAT SHAPE WHO I AM.

I AM CAPABLE OF OVERCOMING ANY
OBSTACLE THAT COMES MY WAY.

I AM WORTHY OF PURSUING MY PASSIONS AND
INTERESTS WITHOUT HESITATION.

I AM PROUD OF MY
ACCOMPLISHMENTS AND USE THEM
AS MOTIVATION TO CONTINUE
GROWING AND EVOLVING.

*I AM CONFIDENT IN MY
ABILITY TO STAND UP FOR
MYSELF AND WHAT I BELIEVE IN.*

OOPS!

I MAY MAKE MISTAKES, BUT I DON'T QUIT.

I MAY STUMBLE, BUT
I NEVER STAY ON THE GROUND

I TRUST IN MY ABILITY TO
LEARN FROM MY MISTAKES AND USE THEM AS
OPPORTUNITIES FOR GROWTH.

I AM PROUD OF MY ABILITY TO RECOGNIZE AND
APPRECIATE MY OWN WORTH.

**I TRUST IN MY ABILITY TO MAKE
MEANINGFUL CONTRIBUTIONS TO THE WORLD.**

I AM DESERVING OF THE SUPPORT AND
ENCOURAGEMENT OF THOSE AROUND ME.

I AM CAPABLE OF ACHIEVING ANYTHING
I SET MY MIND TO WITH
HARD WORK AND DETERMINATION.

I TRUST IN MY INTUITION AND FOLLOW IT WITH COURAGE AND TRUST.

I AM DESERVING OF REST AND RELAXATION, AND TAKE TIME TO RECHARGE AND REJUVENATE.

I AM CONFIDENT IN MY ABILITY TO MAKE DECISIONS THAT ALIGN WITH MY VALUES AND BELIEFS.

I AM CAPABLE OF FINDING JOY AND GRATITUDE IN EVERY MOMENT OF MY LIFE, NO MATTER THE CIRCUMSTANCES.

I AM WORTHY OF RECEIVING LOVE, RESPECT, AND KINDNESS FROM THOSE AROUND ME.

I AM CONFIDENT IN MY ABILITY TO LEARN NEW SKILLS AND EXPAND MY KNOWLEDGE.

I AM DESERVING OF A LIFE FILLED WITH PURPOSE, MEANING AND FULFILLMENT.

I AM CAPABLE OF CREATING A LIFE THAT ALIGNS WITH MY PASSIONS AND DESIRES.

I AM PROUD OF MY ACCOMPLISHMENTS AND CELEBRATE MY SUCCESSES WITH JOY AND GRATITUDE.

I KNOW THESE DREAMS WERE PUT IN
MY HEART FOR A REASON. I TRUST
MY PATH.

*I AM PROUD OF MY INNER
AND OUTER BEAUTY, AND EMBRACE THEM
BOTH WITH LOVE AND ACCEPTANCE.*

*I TRUST IN THE JOURNEY OF MY LIFE,
KNOWING THAT
EVERYTHING HAPPENS
FOR A REASON AND FOR MY HIGHEST GOOD.*

I AM DESERVING OF POSITIVE
AND SUPPORTIVE
RELATIONSHIPS
THAT UPLIFT AND INSPIRE ME.

I AM CAPABLE OF LETTING GO OF ANY
NEGATIVE SELF-TALK
OR LIMITING BELIEFS
THAT HOLD ME BACK.

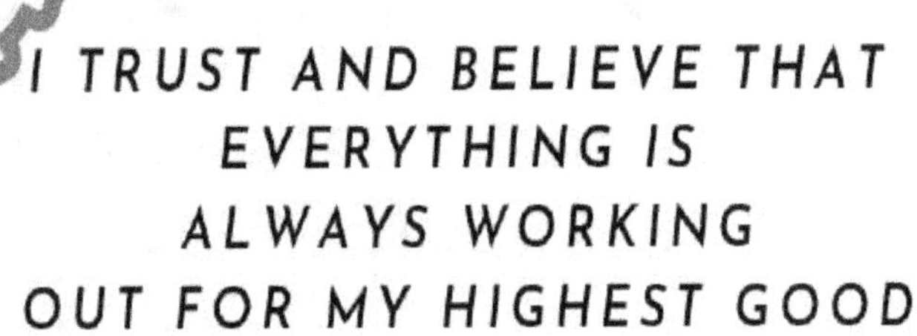

I TRUST AND BELIEVE THAT
EVERYTHING IS
ALWAYS WORKING
OUT FOR MY HIGHEST GOOD

I AM WORTHY OF FORGIVENESS AND RELEASE
ANY GUILT OR SHAME FROM PAST MISTAKES.

I AM CONFIDENT IN MY ABILITY TO
SPEAK MY TRUTH AND
STAND UP FOR MYSELF AND OTHERS.

I USE FAILURE AS A STEPPING TO
SUCCESS.

EVEN WHEN SOMETHING DOESN'T HAPPEN HOW I
WANTED, I KNOW I'M ON THE RIGHT PATH.

I CHOOSE TO FIND HOPEFUL AND
OPTIMISTIC WAYS TO LOOK AT
OBSTACLES AND ROADBLOCKS.

ALL OF MY PROBLEMS HAVE SOLUTIONS.
I RISE IN THE FACE OF ADVERSITY.
I AM RESILIENT.

I SEEK CONNECTION, NOT VALIDATION, FROM OTHERS.

I AM GRATEFUL FOR THE LESSONS AND GROWTH THAT COME FROM DIFFICULT EXPERIENCES.

I AM FREE TO BE MY TRUE AND AUTHENTIC SELF IN ALL MY RELATIONSHIPS.

I FIND LOVE EVERYWHERE I LOOK.

I AM LOVED FOR ALL MY FLAWS AND IMPERFECTIONS.

I AM WORTHY OF BEAUTIFUL FRIENDSHIPS AND LASTING RELATIONSHIPS.

MY FRIENDSHIPS ARE FUN, JOYFUL, AND ROOTED IN PURE, UNCONDITIONAL LOVE.

LOVE IS MY BIRTHRIGHT, AND I WILL NOT SETTLE FOR LESS THAN I DESERVE.

I AM WORTHY OF TRUE AND LASTING LOVE.

I AM WORTHY OF BEING CHERISHED, TREASURED, AND ADORED

NO MATTER WHAT, I ALWAYS DESERVE TO BE
TREATED WITH DIGNITY AND RESPECT.

UNCONDITIONAL LOVE IS MY
BIRTHRIGHT.

I AM FREE TO BE MY
TRUE AND AUTHENTIC SELF IN ALL MY
RELATIONSHIPS.

I AM GRATEFUL FOR THE SUPPORT
AND ENCOURAGEMENT OF THOSE
AROUND ME, AND GIVE THANKS FOR
THEIR PRESENCE IN MY LIFE.

LOVE IS MY BIRTHRIGHT,
AND I WILL NOT SETTLE
FOR LESS THAN I DESERVE.

I AM ON EARTH FOR A REASON, AND I
AM COMMITTED TO LIVING
A POSITIVE LIFE AND BEING A POSITIVE
INFLUENCE ON OTHERS.

LOVE MYSELF AND LIKE MYSELF. I CHOOSE TO
FOCUS ON MY POSITIVE
QUALITIES AND HOW
I CAN USE THEM TO IMPROVE MYSELF AND THE
WORLD.

I ONLY PLANT POSITIVE SEEDS
IN THE WORLD TODAY.
I DO NOT WASTE ONE PRECIOUS
MOMENT IN ANGER, HATRED, OR ENVY.

I ACCEPT THAT I CANNOT CHANGE
THE PAST. I FOCUS ON MY FUTURE
AND MOVE FORWARD
IN MY LIFE.
MY PAST DOES NOT DEFINE WHO I
AM TODAY.

I DO ONE THING EVERY DAY TO MAKE CONSISTENT PROGRESS TOWARD
MY DREAMS.
I SURPASS OTHER PEOPLE'S EXPECTATIONS BECAUSE I AM
EXCEPTIONAL.

EVEN IF I DO SOMETHING WRONG,
I GO BACK AND FIND ANOTHER WAY.
I CREATE A NEW COURSE OF ACTION.
I DO NOT STOP.

I AM READY TO CREATE MORE
SUCCESS IN MY LIFE AND AM READY
TO RELEASE ANY EXCUSES. I AM
PRODUCTIVE AND FOCUSED ON
ATTAINING RESULTS.

I AM OPEN TO ANY NEW OPPORTUNITY THAT COMES MY WAY.
I DO NOT BELIEVE THAT MY OPTIONS ARE LIMITED.

I TRUST MY OWN WISDOM AND INTUITION.
I AM THE ONLY PERSON WHO KNOWS WHAT IS BEST FOR

Thank You

'o all the readers of "Positive Affirmations for Women," thank you for choosing this book to help you cultivate a positive and confident mindset. We hope that the affirmations provided in this book have nspired you to believe in yourself and to pursue your goals with courage and determination. Remember that your thoughts and beliefs shape your reality, and by ısing the affirmations in this book, you can transform your life in powerful and positive ways. We wish you ll the best on your journey towards self-improvement and personal growth.